TARGET Comprehension 2

SKILLS
- Vocabulary
- Reasoning
- Planning
- Summarising
- Word recognition
- Writing ability

Compiled and Edited by: Manpreet Kaur Aden

Illustrated by: Suman S. Roy

Designed by: Rakesh Kumar

Graded • Illustrations & Images • Variety of Genres

All rights are reserved. No part of this book may be reproduced, stored in a retrieval system or transmitted, in any form or by any means, mechanical, photocopying, recording or otherwise, without any prior written permission of the publisher.

1st Impression

© B. Jain Publishers (P) Ltd.

Published by
Kuldeep Jain
for
Pegasus
An imprint of
B. Jain Publishers (P) Ltd.
An ISO 9001 : 2000 Certified Company
1921, Street No. 10, Chuna Mandi, Paharganj, New Delhi-110055 (INDIA)
Tel: 91-11-4567 1000 | Fax: 91-11-4567 1010
Website: **www.bjain.com** | E-mail: **info@bjain.com**

ISBN: 978-81-319-3226-1

Printed in India : JJ Imprints Pvt. Ltd. Noida.

Objectives of Comprehension

It is often seen that whenever children are made to do a comprehension exercise, seldom are they made aware of the purpose of the whole exercise. Many a time, even the guardian or the teacher is not clear about the purpose. Of course, we are all well informed about the common purpose like comprehension teaches a child to maintain his attention and also that it teaches them to use strategies to enhance understanding of the reading material. Given below are some of the common objectives of comprehension:

- *Getting to understand the main idea of the text*
- *Noting the correct sequence of the text*
- *Recognizing the key words of the text*
- *Making reasonable and logical conclusion after reading the text*
- *Recognizing the different genres of the text*
- *Identifying fiction from non-fiction*
- *Distinguishing fantasy from realism*
- *Recognizing the theme, plot and characters of the given passage*

What it is to monitor one's own comprehension?

Children should be trained from a very early age of how to monitor their own comprehension. Sometimes text does not make sense as one reads it and students need to learn to recognize when this happens. At once they should stop to fix it. Students should stop regularly and check while reading to make sure that they understand what they are reading. Reread and think again and again. They should read to the end of the page, think, and see if they are still confused. Learn the strategy of decoding multi-syllabic words. The students should be able to summarize a variety of written texts.

This series **Target Comprehension** is an excellently planned and graded series which brings together a diverse range of passages for the children to read. All the reading material that occurs in this book are judged on the basis of theme, language and the overall readability of the passages. The activities are graded too and fit in justly with the passages.

Contents

1. The Three Billy Goats 6
2. The Frogs ask for a King 12
3. The Canary 17
4. Ice Cream 21
5. Forests 26
6. The Farmer and his Sons 31
7. The Princess and the Pea 35
8. Blue Whale 41
9. Walt Disney 47
10. The Bremen Town Musicians 53
11. The Gift of Pearls 59
12. Deserts 64
13. Bed in Summer 68
14. Roller Skates 73
15. Earthquake 79
16. Little Red Hen 84

Fun to Know

A warming up discussion

Do you like to travel?

Name one place which you wish to visit.

The Three Billy Goats

Once upon a time there were three Billy goats who were brothers. The eldest one was called Great Big Billy Goat, the second one Big Billy Goat and the youngest one was called Little Billy Goat.

The three Billy Goats lived happily in a meadow by the side of a cliff. On the other side of the cliff a winding river flowed. Beyond the river was a lush green meadow.

The Little Billy Goat wanted to go to the meadow. 'Brother, can't we go to the meadow and eat the green grass that grows there?' he asked. 'But for that we have to cross the old wooden bridge over the river,' said the eldest Billy Goat. 'Let me go first,' said the Little Billy Goat, excitedly.

Now, a huge, ugly Troll lived under the wooden bridge. He had saucer like eyes and a poker like nose. Whenever, someone wanted to cross the bridge, they had to take his permission. And instead of giving permission, he ate them up!

Little Billy Goat was unaware of this. He stepped onto the bridge and trip, trap, he trotted. 'WHO IS TRIPPING ON MY BRIDGE?' roared the Troll. Startled, the Little Billy Goat replied in a feeble voice, 'It is I, Little Billy Goat. I am going to the meadow.'

'No, you will not go anywhere as I will eat you!' said the Troll. 'Please do not eat me,' cried Little Billy Goat. 'I am too small and thin. I won't be able to fill your stomach. Wait for Big Billy Goat who is coming after me. He is much bigger than me.'

'Well, then get off my bridge quickly,' thundered the Troll.

And so, Little Billy Goat crossed the bridge safely. After a while, Big Billy Goat stepped on the bridge, trip trapping! Once again the Troll roared, 'WHO IS TRIPPING ON MY BRIDGE?' 'It is I, Big Billy Goat going up to the meadow,' he said, loudly.

'No, you won't. I am coming to gobble you up, Big Billy Goat,' boomed the Troll. 'Please, don't eat me as I am not big enough to fill your stomach,' pleaded Big Billy Goat. 'Wait, till the Great Big Billy Goat crosses the bridge. He is bigger than me.' Again, the Troll agreed and let him pass.

Soon, Great Big Billy Goat stepped on the bridge. Trip, trap! Trip, trap! Trip, trap!

Now, Great Big Billy Goat was so heavy that the bridge creaked and groaned under his weight. Suddenly, a large pair of round eyes peeped from beneath the bridge.

'WHO IS TRYING TO BREAK MY BRIDGE?' yelled the Troll.

'IT'S ME, GREAT BIG BILLY GOAT!' he replied, in a hoarse voice. 'Wait! I am coming to eat you up,' roared the Troll. 'Well, come along!' muttered the Great Big Billy Goat and lowered his horns preparing to butt the Troll.

The next moment, the ugly Troll stepped on the bridge.

He looked at Great Big Billy Goat and then charged at him furiously. But Great Big Billy Goat was prepared. WHAM! He bumped into the Troll and threw him up into the air. The Troll circled in the air a few times and fell into the river with a crash! Then, Great Big Billy Goat crossed the bridge and went to the meadow to join his brothers.

Happily, they ate the lovely green grass in the meadow and the red, juicy apples growing there. And now they could also walk over the bridge whenever they wished to.

Let's remember the story

1. Where did the Little Billy Goat want to go?
2. Who lived under the bridge?
3. What did the goats want to eat in the meadow?
4. What sound did the goats make when they crossed the bridge?
5. Who butted the Troll?
6. Who had saucer like eyes?

Find friends

Some words are given below in two columns. These words are called **rhyming words** because when you speak them, their ends sound the same. Read these words aloud and match each word with its friend.

Column A	Column B
Green	Flash
Cliff	Queen
Poker	Door
Cross	Joker
Roar	Stiff
Crash	Moss

Practice writing sentences

A few words are given below. Can you make small sentences using the given words?

1. Goat

2. Big

3. River

4. Little

5. Green

6. Round

Read aloud

Read the passage given below aloud.

Green is a beautiful colour! The grass that you walk on is green and the leaves of the trees are also green. Most plants and trees are green too! Frogs are green and so are grasshoppers.

Did you know that you can make green colour by mixing blue and yellow? As you have made the colour green my mixing two primary colours, it is called a secondary colour. Green is also used to show things that do not harm the Earth. Green things are made from reused materials which are safe to throw out in the trash.

For the teacher

As this passage has many words that begin with 'gr' sound, the teacher can take this opportunity to brush up the 'gr' sound.

Fun to Know

2 **A warming up discussion**
Do you pray? Why?
What do you pray about?

The Frogs ask for a King

Long ago, a colony of frogs lived in a pond in a forest. They, however, had no king. So, one day, a group of frogs went to God Jupiter asking for a king. After listening to their plea, God Jupiter said, 'Return home and you shall soon have a king.' Happily the frogs returned.

The next day, Jupiter threw a log into the pool. The log fell with a loud splash frightening the frogs who hid inside the pool. When however the log stayed still for a few minutes, the frogs rushed up to it.

Soon, the frogs realized that the log was their king. The frogs were happy for they now had a king.

After a while, the frogs thought that their king wasn't good. It was because the log did not do anything. It just stayed still. So, they once again returned to God Jupiter asking for a ruler. Once again, God Jupiter agreed to grant their wish. This time, he sent an eel to govern the frogs. But soon, the frogs began disliking the eel for he was kind and just.

A third time, the frogs went to God Jupiter. By now, God Jupiter was angry with their repeated complaints. He understood that the frogs would not be satisfied by whichever king he sent them. So, he decided to punish them. This time, he sent a heron as their ruler. From that day, God Jupiter heard no complaints from the frogs. How could the frogs complain, the heron ate a frog each day until not a single frog was left to complain!

Let's remember the story

1. Who wanted a king?
2. Whom did the frogs go to?
3. Why were the frogs frightened?
4. Why were the frogs unhappy with their king?
5. Why was God Jupiter angry?
6. Why were the frogs unable to complain when the heron became their king?

Jumbled sentences

Rearrange the words given below to make meaningful sentences.

1. pond/ are/ the/ swans/ in/ swimming

2. is/ Sharon/ in/ park/ skating/ the

3. is /Toby/ the/ climbing/ tree

4. is/ the/ dog/ butterfly/ the/ catching

5. many/ there/ the/ flowers/ are/ in/ vase

6. loudly/ is/ the/ crowing/ rooster

Finding the nouns

Circle all the common nouns in the sentences given below.

1. The birds collected straw to make their nest.

2. I have a dog and four birds as my pet.

3. The flower shop is in the corner.

4. Martha is wearing a raincoat and has an umbrella.

5. The teacher asked her student a question.

6. Grandfather kept his book on the table.

One and more

Read the words given below. Can you make plurals of the given words?

Singular	Plural
King	
Day	
Wish	
Book	
Ruler	
Colony	

Can you guess the letter?

The words given below are incomplete. Would you complete them?

J_P_TE_	CO__NY
_EA__ZE	SPL__H
C__PL_IN	A__RY

Fun to Know

A warming up discussion
Did you have a pet?
How did you take care of it?

The Canary

Elizabeth Turner

Mary had a little bird,
With feathers bright and yellow,
Slender legs-upon my word,
He was a pretty fellow!
Sweetest notes he always sung,
Which much delighted Mary;
Often where his cage was hung,
She sat to hear Canary.
Crumbs of bread and dainty seeds
She carried to him daily,
Seeking for the early weeds,
She decked his palace gaily.
This, my little readers, learn,
And ever practice duly;
Songs and smiles of love return
To friends who love you truly.

Find friends

Some words are given below in two columns. These words are called **rhyming words** because when you speak them, their ends sound the same. Read these words aloud and match each word with its friend.

Column A	Column B
Bright	Page
Cage	Head
Seed	Brittle
Bird	Night
Bread	Read
Little	Word

Let's remember the story

1. Who had a little bird?
2. Give two words that tell us about the feathers of the bird.
3. When was Mary delighted?
4. What kind of bird did Mary have?
5. What did the bird eat?
6. What does the word 'palace' mean in the poem?

Knowing your pet!

You must have a pet. Tell us about your pet.

 **Can you guess the word?**

The words given below are incomplete. Would you complete them?

C _ N _ RY

FR _ E _ D _

C _ _ E

SLE _ _ E _

CR _ _ B

F _ _ T _ ER

Fun to Know

A warming up discussion

Which is your favourite ice cream?
Do you know who first made ice creams?

Ice Cream

Ice cream was first made many hundreds of years ago. It is found that the first ice cream was made when the Roman Emperor Nero asked his cooks to make a cold dessert. The cooks then had ice brought from the mountains and grated it. They then presented this ice with many fruit toppings to the emperor. This was the first ice cream. Then, a Chinese king used to eat combinations of ice and milk. This was another kind of ice cream.

Many, many years later, the recipes to make ice cream were brought from China to Europe. In Europe ice creams were made using ice with fruits, milk and sherbets. During this time, ice cream was eaten by only the kings and other important people. At last, the ice cream recipes came to the

United States. It was here that ice cream became what it is today.

People learnt how to make ice creams and began making it. Some people even opened small ice cream parlours selling ice creams. Ice cream became popular and they were even given for free.

The first ice cream parlour in America was opened in New York City in 1776. This was also the first time that the word 'ice cream' was used. By now, the way an ice cream was made had changed a lot. By now, ice used to make ice cream was mixed with salt to lower and control the temperature of ingredients of the ice cream. This method greatly improved the way ice cream was made. During this time, the invention of wooden bucket freezer with rotary paddles had also made the manufacture of ice cream better. Slowly, ice cream became more popular. Then, Augustus Jackson, a confectionery owner from Philadelphia, thought of many new recipes for making ice cream in 1832.

Later, in 1846, Nancy Johnson invented the hand-cranked freezer. Then, in 1851, Jacob Fussell in Baltimore established the first large-scale commercial ice cream plant. That was the beginning of the making of ice creams on a large scale all over the world.

Complete the sentences

Read the sentences given below. Choose the correct word from the bracket to complete the sentences.

1. Emperor………… (Zero/Nero) tasted the first ice cream.
2. Chinese king's ice cream had ice and……… (silk/ milk).
3. Fruits and……… (water/ sherbets) were also used to make ice cream.
4. Only……. (soldiers/ kings) ate the ice cream.
5. To lower the temperature of ice cream……… (sand/ salt) was used.
6. Jacob Fussell made the first…………. (ice cream/ sugar) plant.

One and more

Read the words given below. Can you make plurals of the given words?

Singular	Plural
Cook	
Fruit	
Milk	
City	
Plant	
Year	

Pair and share

Work in group and ask your partner which is his/ her favourite ice cream. Ask them what flavour it is, what colour is it and why do they like it! Then you can read it with the help of your teacher.

g Circling the words

Read the sentences given below. Put a circle around all those words that are opposites to each other.

1. Ice is **cold** but the coffee is **hot**.
2. Megan is **tall** while Suzy is **short**.
3. The cat is **fat** while the dog is **thin**.
4. I kept my **new** pencil with the **old** ones.
5. Ryan is **happy** but Bob is **sad**.
6. The elephant is **big** but the ant is **small**.

 My favourite ice cream

Write 3 sentences about your favourite ice cream.

Fun to Know

A warming up discussion

Have you seen a forest?
What did you see there?

Forests

A forest is a large area of land that is covered with thousands of trees and shrubs. About one third of the earth's surface is covered with forests. Trees in a forest are very closely placed. Sometimes, due to the closeness of the trees, the sunlight does not even reach the forest floor! Forests are found all over the world. They are also home to a large number of birds and animals. Some birds and animals may be found in one type of forest.

There are different types of forests all over the world. The climate and soil of a region determines what type of a forest would be in a particular area.

Forests are of various types—tropical rainforests, temperate rainforests, boreal forests and mangrove forests. All these forests look different because of the climate and the soil of where they are located.

Tropical rainforests are very dense. These forests are warm, wet and it rains almost daily in such forests. Temperate rainforests are the most colourful of the forests. These forests are also called deciduous forests. The leaves in these forests change colour during autumn, they fall in winter and they grow again in spring.

Boreal forests are also evergreen forests. These forests have a cold and harsh climate. Lastly, mangrove forests are seen at the mouth of large rivers. These forests do not allow the soil to move. They also make the flow of water slow.

Forests are a huge source of fresh air. The forests also keep the climate in check as they do not allow too many harmful gases to remain in the atmosphere. Did you know that the canopy, the topmost layer of the forest, is so thick in rainforests that rainfall takes 10 minutes to reach the ground! All of us also depend on the forests for wood, paper, rubber, food and even medicines! Forests are therefore very, very important for our survival.

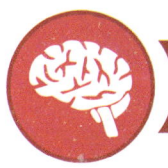 **Let's remember the story**

1. What is a forest?
2. Why can't sunlight enter forests easily?
3. Name any two types of forests.
4. How long does it take rainfall to reach the floor ground? Why?
5. Which forests are called deciduous forests?
6. Name a few things that we get from the forests.

Find friends

Some words are given below in two columns. These words are called **rhyming words** because when you speak them, their ends sound the same. Read these words aloud and match each word with its friend.

Column A	Column B
Tree	Snore
Floor	Grain
Soil	Form
Dense	Free
Warm	Fence
Rain	Boil

Complete the sentences

Choose the correct word from the bracket and complete the sentences.

1. A forest has lots of trees and.............. (water/ shrubs).
2. The sunlight does not reach the forest................ (floor/ top).
3. Tropical rainforests are.............. (open/ dense).
4. Leaves in temperate rainforests change their............ (colour/ look).
5. Forests are a source of.............. (stale/ fresh) air.
6. The topmost layer of a forest is called.............. (peak/ canopy).

Jumbled sentences

The words in the sentences below are not in their right order. Can you put them in the right order to make meaningful sentences?

1. are/ forests/ dense/ very

2. forests/ many/ live/ in/ birds

3. the/ we/ wood/ get/ forest/ from

4. in/ most/ live/ animals/ forests

5. give/ air/ forests/ fresh/ us

6. world/ are/ forests/ the/ all/ over

Group activity

 **Planting a tree!**

The teacher will take the children to the school garden. There with the help of the teacher, the children will plant seeds. The teacher can tell them about seeds and how plants grow out of them. The teacher can also take a coloured picture of a plant complete with its roots to make children understand how plants grow.

Fun to Know

6 **A warming up discussion**

Who is a farmer? • What does a farmer do?

The Farmer and his Sons

Once there lived an old man in a certain village. The old man had worked hard all his life but his three sons liked to remain idle. The old man worried what would happen to his farm after he died. One day, the farmer had an idea how to make his sons start working.

The farmer called his sons one morning and said, 'Sons, I have to tell you a secret. A great treasure is hidden in our farm. You must dig for it after I die.' The sons were delighted hearing about the treasure. Some days later the old farmer died. Soon, the old man's sons thought of bringing home the treasure from the farm.

The sons, then, picked up their spades and mattocks and went to their farm. Soon, they had dug the whole farm. But where was the treasure! 'All our efforts have gone in vain,' said the youngest brother. The brothers were disappointed. 'We have dug the soil, we now might as well sow the seeds,' suggested the eldest among them.

And so they did. With time, the brothers had a good crop. The brothers then cut the harvest and sold it in the market with great profit. It was then that the brothers understood that it was this treasure that their father had talked about. Ever since that day, the brothers worked hard on the farm and each year they found great treasure in their farm.

Let's remember the story

1. Why was the old man worried?
2. What was hidden in the farm?
3. What did the sons pick up?
4. What did they find in the farm?
5. What did the brothers decide to sow?
6. What was the treasure?

Gender bender

Can you give the opposite gender of the given words?

Column A	Column B
Man	
Boy	
Son	

Brother	
King	
Uncle	

Practice writing sentences

A few words are given below. Can you make small sentences using the given words?

1. Man

2. Farm

3. Brother

4. Hard

5. Morning

6. Market

_____

Read aloud

Read the passage given below aloud.

Penguins are among the most popular birds. Penguins are only found in Antarctica. They are of many different kinds. Emperor Penguins are the largest penguins. And the smallest penguins are Little Blue Penguins. Penguins are birds but they cannot fly.

Penguins live on the coldest and the windiest climate on Earth. So, they have a thick layer of fat on their bodies to protect them from the cold. Did you know that penguins can swim very well! They can even swim very fast and they can make deep dives in the sea. Penguins eat fish.

Fun to Know

A warming up discussion

Can a small pea hurt you?

What will happen if peas were kept in the bed you sleep in?

The Princess and the Pea

The happenings in this story took place long, long ago. In a certain kingdom, a prince was looking for a princess to marry. But he wasn't looking for any princess. He wanted to marry a Real princess!

The prince travelled to many kingdoms, far and wide, in search of a real princess. But no matter which princess he met, he didn't found her to be the real princess.

So, after a long and disappointing search for the real princess, the prince returned to his kingdom. When his parents saw him sad, they tried to cheer him up. But their efforts went in vain.

Some time passed by. One evening, there came a terrible storm. 'Oh my!' said the queen, 'I have never seen such a frightening storm.' 'It indeed is frightening,' agreed the king, as he stood with the queen by the castle window.

'Did someone knock on the castle door?' asked the queen after a while. The king too heard distant knocking on the castle door. 'Dear, I will go and see,' he said.

When the king reached the castle door, the knocking on the door had become frantic. The king opened the metal doors and then gasped!

'Goodness gracious!' cried the king. 'What could you possibly be doing in this dreadful weather, my dear?' A girl dressed in royal clothes and wearing a small crown stood at the door. Her dripping wet dress had created a pool of water at her feet and her hair was stuck to her forehead!

'I had gone out to meet a cousin when this dreadful storm started,' said the girl. 'And before long I looked like this.' 'Who are you, young lady?' asked the king. 'I am a princess…a real princess,' said the girl.

'Could she really be a real princess?' wondered the king. But he hastily led the princess inside the castle as she had started shivering from cold. He then rushed to bring the queen.

After listening to everything, the queen said, 'We will soon find out if she is a real princess.' She came downstairs with the king and asked the princess to warm herself by the fireplace while she prepared a bed for her to sleep in.

The queen instructed two maids, 'Prepare the guest room. Put twenty mattresses and twenty eider-down blankets on the bed for the princess to sleep in.'

The maids began their work. But the moment, the maid took off the bedding the queen put a pea on the bed. 'Now put the mattresses and the eider-down blankets on it,' said the queen.

Soon, the princess came to the guest room. 'Sleep well, my dear,' said the queen and left the room. The princess then climbed on the bed and lay down on it.

Next morning, the queen came to the princess. 'Good morning, my dear,' said the queen. 'I hope that you slept well.' 'Your Highness,' said the princess looking miserable, 'I did not sleep well at all. I felt as if a rock had been kept in the bed. My whole body aches.'

The queen was overjoyed to hear this. The girl standing before her was indeed a real princess! When the prince heard about this, he was so happy.

Some time later a grand wedding took place in the castle. The prince and the princess were happy. The celebrations went on for days. However, after this wedding other princes too started looking for their real princesses! Those stories can certainly wait.

 **Let's remember the story**

1. Why was the prince disappointed?
2. When did the princess come to the king's castle?
3. Who she had gone to meet?
4. How many mattresses were kept on the princess' bed?
5. What did the queen put under the mattresses?
6. Why were the king and queen happy?

g Circling the words

Read the sentences given below. Put a circle around all those word that are opposites of each other.

1. Father goes out by day and comes back at night.

2. The bird is heavy but its feathers are light.

3. Father is going up the stairs, Sue is coming down.

4. The deserts are dry but oceans are wet.

5. The boy is young and his grandfather is old.

6. The tortoise is slow and the rabbit is fast.

One and more

Read the words given below. Can you make plurals of the given words?

Singular	Plural
Prince	
Castle	
Marry	
Room	
Sleep	
Rock	

Complete the sentences

Read the sentences given below. Complete the sentences by choosing the correct words.

1. Kites .... (skip/fly) in the sky.

2. The king is coming to his .... (river/castle).

3. The girls are skipping over a .... (cards/rope).

4. The sun rises in the .... (morning/evening).

5. There are many .... (moon/stars) in the sky at night.

6. The fish swim in the .... (sky/water).

Fun to Know

8

A warming up discussion

Which is the biggest animal you have seen?
Where does that animal live?

Blue Whale

Blue Whales are the largest animals on Earth. This amazing animal is very, very long. Well, if you can make 33 grown elephants stand back to back that will give you some idea how big a grown whale is! Blue Whale's heart is as big as a small car.

It does not eat large animals to grow so big. Instead, it feeds on very small shrimp-like creatures called krill. And a whale eats a large house full of krill each day!

Blue Whales do not have teeth. In place of teeth, they have baleen. Baleen are fringed plates of a material that is a bit similar to the material that makes up your fingernails. It is attached to its upper jaw. This huge animal gulps lots of water which is then taken into its belly. In this process, the krill get caught in the baleen which are eaten and the water is pushed out.

Blue Whales look true blue underwater but on the surface their colouring is more of a mottled blue-gray. The Blue Whale has a broad, flat head and a long, tapered body that ends in wide, triangular flukes.

Blue Whales live in all the world's oceans. They are sometimes seen in groups, sometimes in pairs but usually alone. They often go during the summer time to feed in polar waters. During winters, the Blue Whale goes towards the equator. These long distance journeys take place each year.

How loud can you shout? Perhaps your shout can be heard a few metres away. A Blue Whale on the other hand is also the loudest animal on the earth. Their sounds can be heard 1,000 miles away! In this manner, it can talk with its friends and family which are many miles away.

Can you guess how big a Blue Whale calf can be when it is born? Well, a baby blue whale at the time of its birth is the largest baby in the world. It is only a little bit smaller than your school bus! And it grows to be as huge as its mother in a few years.

Blue Whales are also among Earth's longest-lived animals. They can live to be very old about more than 100 years.

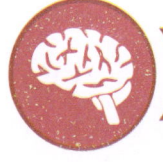

Let's remember the story

1. How large is a Blue Whale's heart?
2. What do the Blue Whale has in its mouth in place of teeth?
3. What colour do the Blue Whale appear to be when it comes on surface?
4. Where does the Blue Whale go in summer and in winter?
5. How far can a Blue Whale be heard?
6. Why do the Blue Whales shout so loudly?

Crossword

With the help of the given clues complete the following crossword.

Across

1. It is cold in this season
2. It is the colour of water and sky

Down

3. It is the biggest animal in the world
4. It stops at a bus stop
5. A large body of salty water
6. A small water animal which many people eat

Practice writing sentences

A few words are given below. Can you make small sentences using the given words?

1. Blue

2. Long

3. Eat

4. Big

5. Water

6. Hand

Find friends

Some words are given below in two columns. These words are called **rhyming words** because when you speak them, their ends sound the same. Read these words aloud and match each word with its friend.

Column A	Column B
Blue	Walk
Long	Deer
Year	Mouse
Loud	Song
Talk	Shoe
House	Cloud

Jumbled words

The letters in the words given below are misplaced. Place the letters in their correct order to make meaningful words.

HWLAE ....

MRHISP ....

RILKL ....

EAENBL ....

ARLETGS ....

GOLNETS ....

Fun to Know

A warming up discussion
Which is your favourite cartoon?
Have you ever tried drawing a cartoon?

Walt Disney

Walt Disney was born on December 5, 1901 in Chicago, Illinois. Elias Disney was his father and Flora Call Disney was his mother. Walt was one of five children of his parents. After Walt's birth, the Disney family moved to Marceline Missouri. Here they lived in a farmhouse. Walt spent his childhood here and he enjoyed himself greatly.

From his childhood Walt wanted to have everyone's attention. He was seven years old when he first went to school. At school, he always wanted to keep everyone happy. Once, he even took a field mouse, which he had caught, to school. He had put a leash on the field mouse using a thread. Though he was punished for bringing the mouse but Walt had been able to entertain the other children. Little did he know that many years later, another mouse will make him world famous.

From his childhood, Walt used to draw. He even made drawings for his neighbours to get pocket money. Though his father was strict, his mother and elder brother Roy knew that Walt was talented and they encouraged him. Once, he even made drawings on the back of their house using tar. When his family moved again, he attended McKinley High School in Chicago where he studied art and photography.

During the fall of 1918, Disney tried to enter into military service. But as he was underage at 16 years, he was refused. He then joined the Red Cross and was sent to France. He stayed for a year in France driving an ambulance. But his ambulance unlike the other ambulances was covered with cartoons made by Disney.

When he returned, Walt decided to start his career. He started a small company called Laugh-O-Grams but he soon had to close the company. But he had not lost hope. He took a suitcase and twenty dollars with him and came to Hollywood.

He worked hard and made a cartoon series called **Alice Comedies**. The cartoon series was a great success. He went on to make other cartoon characters. Then in 1928, he released **Steamboat Willie**. It was a cartoon with sound. This was the first time that **Mickey Mouse** was seen. The cartoon was a great success.

In 1932, he made **Flowers and Trees** which was the first colour cartoon. This cartoon also won him an Academy Award. But it was in 1937 that Walt Disney changed the way cartoons were made. He had released a full length cartoon feature film. **Snow White and the Seven Dwarfs** which went on to become a huge classic. It was just a beginning for he went on to make more animated feature films including **Pinocchio, Dumbo** and **Bambi**.

As animated feature films had become a success, Walt Disney started thinking of making a clean and organized amusement park. He wanted to make a park where children and adults could meet their favourite characters. This park was Walt Disney's dream. And then in 1955 Disneyland Park was opened. He had many other dreams as well. Some of which were completed only after he had died.

Walt Disney died in 1966. After he died, his brother Roy continued to fulfill his dreams. Walt Disney was a remarkable man who brought happiness into everyone's life. He told us about stories that had happened in the past but through his stories, he had showed us the future. It is through the world which he had created that Walt Disney will always be remembered.

Complete the sentences

Read the sentences given below and complete them.

1. One day, Walt Disney brought to his school.................................... He was .... for it.

2. Walt made drawing for his neighbours to get..

3. He joined Red Cross and was sent........................ On his ambulance he...............................

4. Steamboat Willie was the first cartoon..................................... It was the first time...

5. He also made a full length feature film. The first film he made was............ ....

6. He also wanted to open an amusement park where the children .... So, he opened ....

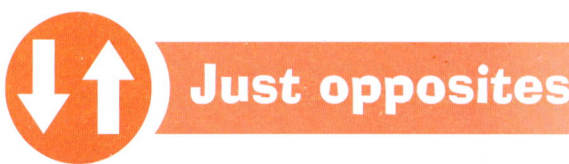

Just opposites

Think and write the correct opposite of the words given below.

1. Old

2. Happy

3. Back

4. Start

5. First

6. Clean

Practice writing sentences

A few words are given below. Can you make small sentences using the given words?

1. First

2. School

3. Mouse

4. Small

5. Park

6. Clean

 **Jumbled sentences**

The sentences below do not have the words in the right order. Can you put the words correctly and make meaningful sentences.

1. made/ Tom/ cartoon/ a

2. cap/ wore/ new/ Clara/ a

6. into/ boy/ puddle/ fell/ a/ the

4. sandwich/ ate/ a/ big/ Joey

5. chocolate/ made/ mother/ cake/ a

6. cleaning/ is/ car/ the/ father

Cartoon talk!

Let us encourage children to speak. The teacher will ask the students to think for five minutes about their favourite cartoon characters. Then, one by one a child will come in front of the class and talk about his/her favourite cartoon character.

Fun to Know

A warming up discussion

Have you ever travelled to another town/city?
What will you do if robbers caught you on the way?

The Bremen Town Musicians

In a distant land, a man had a donkey who served him for many years carrying sacks to the mill. But now the donkey had grown old. His master thought that it was useless feeding him. Fearing that he would be killed, the donkey ran away. He went towards Bremen thinking to become a town musician.

A few miles later, he saw a hunting dog lying at the road side looking tired.

'Why do you look so sad, my friend?' asked the donkey.

'I am a hunting dog. When I could no longer hunt, my master wanted to kill me. I ran away. But what about food?' said the dog.

'I have an idea,' said the donkey, thoughtfully. 'Come with me to Bremen and be a musician. I'll play the lute and you can beat the drums.'

'I will go with you,' said the dog, happily.

It didn't take long before they came to a cat who was sitting sadly by the roadside. 'What has happened my dear friend?' asked the donkey, kindly.

'I am getting old. I cannot chase mice as I used to do earlier. So my mistress wanted to drown me but I ran away. But where will I go now?'

'Come with us to Bremen. You can become a town musician there,' said the donkey. The cat agreed and went along.

Soon, the trio came to a farmyard where a rooster sat crowing loudly.

'Why are you crowing so loudly?' asked the donkey.

'Tomorrow, the guests are coming. The landlady wants me to be cooked. So I am supposed to let them kill me this evening. That's why I'm crowing as loudly as I can,' said the rooster, sadly.

'My dear Red Head come with us. We're going to Bremen. You have a good voice and we can make music together,' said the dog.

The rooster was happy and agreed. And so, all the four friends went off together.

Towards evening, they reached a forest. They decided to spend the night there. The donkey and the dog lay down under a big tree and the cat rested in the branches. The rooster flew right to the top so that he could see far off things.

Before falling asleep the rooster looked around and saw a little spark burning at a distance. 'I think there is a house nearby,' he said.

The donkey said, 'Then we must get up and go there.'

So, they all moved forward towards the place where the light was. Soon they came to an old cottage. As the donkey was the tallest among them, he looked through the window. All his friends eagerly waited for him.

'Friend, what do you see? asked the rooster excitedly.

'I see a table set with delicious food and four robbers enjoying themselves,' answered the donkey.

'I am sure there will be something for us! Why don't we drive those robbers away?' suggested the rooster.

Then the four friends thought of a plan to drive away the robbers. According to their plan, the donkey stood on the window with his front feet, the dog jumped on the donkey's back, the cat climbed onto the dog, and finally the rooster flew up and sat on the cat! Then, they began to call out together. The donkey BRAYED, the dog BARKED, the cat MEOWED

and the rooster CROWED. Then they crashed through the window into the room shattering the panes! The robbers fled into the woods in great fear crying, 'Ghost! Ghost!' When the robbers were gone, the four friends merrily feasted on the food.

When the four friends had eaten their fill, they went to sleep. The donkey lay down in the farmyard, the dog behind the door, the cat on the hearth and the rooster sat on the beam of the roof. Soon they fell asleep. Later that night, the robbers saw that all was quiet in the cottage. So, they sent a robber to the cottage.

The robber went into the kitchen to strike a light. But hearing his footsteps the cat woke up. The robber mistook the cat's glowing eyes for burning coals. He held a match to them. Angry, the cat scratched his face badly.

Frightened, he ran towards the back door. Meanwhile, the others had woken up too. So, when he came to the back door, the dog bit him in the leg. In the yard, the donkey kicked him hard and the rooster cried, 'Cock-a-doodle-doo!'

The robber ran to his friends and said, 'Oh, there is a horrible WITCH in the house! She scratched my face with her long nails and also bit me in the leg. A black monster in the yard struck me with its club. And the judge sitting up on the roof called out, 'Bring the rogue here!' I ran away as fast as I could.'

The robbers didn't return to the cottage and the four friends lived there happily.

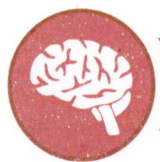 **Let's remember the story**

1. Where did the donkey want to go and why?
2. Who became the singer of the group?
3. What did the rooster see in the forest?
4. Who was eating food inside the cottage?
5. Who did the robbers think had come to their cottage?
6. What happened when the robber lit a match?

Find friends

Some words are given below in two columns. These words are called **rhyming words** because when you speak them, their ends sound the same. Read these words aloud and match each word with its friend.

Column A	Column B
Town	Rice
Mice	Free
Tree	Pitch
Light	Neat
Feet	Down
Witch	Night

Complete the sentences

Read the passage given below. Choose the correct words from the brackets to fill in the blanks.

It was a Sunday. Ryan went to the............... (beach/park) with his father, mother and younger sister. On the beach they wore swimming suits. Then, Ryan went........................ (swimming/talking) with his father in the......... (rocks/ sea). After some time, he collected............ (water/rocks) in a small bucket. He took a shovel and dug into the sand. His sister helped him too. They soon made a sand.................... (home/ castle). Then, his sister collected............... (crabs/ seashells) with Ryan. After some time, Ryan's mother called them. They ate sandwiches and drank............. (tea/ juice). Ryan had a great time on the beach.

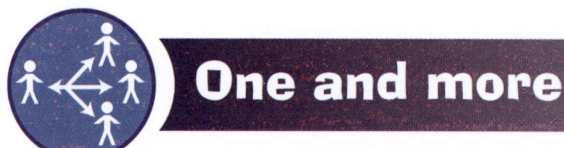

One and more

Read the words given below. Can you make plurals of the given words?

Singular	Plural
Mile	
Mouse	
Cook	
Branch	
Table	
Roof	

Fun to Know

A warming up discussion

Are you kind to your brothers and sisters?
What will you do if pearls fell out of your mouth when you talked?

The Gift of Pearls

Characters:

Narrator   Mother   Georgiana

Rosy   Old woman

Script

Narrator: Long ago, there lived a woman who had two daughters—Georgiana and Rosy. Both her daughters were beautiful. But Georgiana, the eldest was proud while Rosy was kind and gentle.

Georgiana: (before the mirror) I am so beautiful. I shall only marry a prince.

Narrator: No prince came yet to marry her. Time passed.

Mother: Rosy! Where are you? Who will clean the house? And cook our food!

Rosy: I am coming mother after I put the clothes on the clothesline.

Narrator: So, Rosy worked all day while her mother and Georgiana sat and talked. One day, when Rosy went to bring water, she saw an old woman sitting by the well.

Old woman: My dear, I am very thirsty. I cannot draw water from the well. Will you give me some water?

Rosy: I shall draw water for you right away.

Narrator: Rosy drew water from the well and the old woman drank the water to her heart's content.

Old woman: My dear, you have been kind to me. So, I bless you that pearls will fall from your mouth whenever you shall speak.

Narrator: Saying so, the woman went away. Meanwhile, Rosy drew water once more, filled her container with it and went home.

Mother: Why are you so late? We are starving here!

Rosy: Mother, I met an old woman who was…

Narrator: Before Rosy could say another word pearls fell down from her mouth. Rosy was surprised. Her mother and sister Georgiana were shocked. Then, Rosy told them about the old woman and her blessing as pearls kept falling from her mouth.

Mother: Georgiana, you must go and find this old woman. Tomorrow, you shall bring water.

Georgiana: I will mother. Perhaps, diamonds will fall from my mouth when I shall speak.

Narrator: So, the next day, Georgiana went to fetch water from the well. To her delight, she saw an old woman sitting by the well.

Old woman: My dear, would you draw some water for me. I am thirsty.

Georgiana: Yes, I will.

Narrator: But as the old woman began to drink water, she spilled some water on Georgiana's dress.

Georgiana: You have spoiled my silk dress, clumsy old woman!

Old woman: You are so rude, young lady. As your punishment, frogs will come out of your mouth every time you shall speak.

Narrator: Crying Georgiana came back home.

Georgiana: Mother! Mother!

Narrator: The next moment, frogs came out of her mouth and she cried harder. She told her mother all that had happened. Soon, there were many frogs on the floor.

Mother: What have you done? Why could you not leave your pride aside? What will happen now?

Georgiana: Mother, I shall change my behaviour and be kind. Perhaps in this manner, my punishment will end.

Rosy: And I shall help you dear sister.

Narrator: So, from that day, Georgiana changed her ways. She worked with her sister. And one day, no frog dropped from her mouth. Her punishment had ended. Georgiana was happy. Since that day, she had been living happily with her sister and mother.

 **Let's remember the story**

1. Who wanted to marry a prince?
2. What did the old woman ask Rosy to do?
3. How did the old woman bless Rosy?
4. Why did Georgiana want to go to bring water?
5. How was Georgiana punished?
6. How did Georgiana's punishment end?

 **Gender bender**

Can you give the opposite gender of the given words?

Column A	Column B
Mother	
Woman	
Daughter	
Girl	
Princess	
Lady	

 **Practice writing sentences**

Make sentences of the words given below.

1. Kind

2. Food

3. Woman

4. Frog

5. Home

6. Thirsty

 **Let's act**

The teacher should help the children present a skit on the story 'The geese and the tortoise'. The teacher can write the script and the children will enact it.

Fun to Know

12 **A warming up discussion**
Have you heard about a place that is filled with sand?
Have you seen such a place?

Deserts

A desert is a long stretch of land that is covered with sand. It is a dry piece of land because it has very little water in it. A desert has very little or no rain. And so, it is very hot in a desert. It also has a small amount of plants in it which are mainly cactus. Do you know that about one-fifth of the earth's surface is covered with deserts!

Deserts are found on every continent of the world. It can be of many kinds. A desert can be made up of only sand or it can be rocky. There are even cold deserts. Cold deserts have a vast stretch of land that is covered with snow!

The largest hot desert in the world is the Sahara Desert. It is filled with hundreds of sand dunes. Sand dunes are full of sand. Sometimes, these sand dunes can be very big. During the day, a desert is very, very hot while it is cold at night. Only a few animals live in this harsh atmosphere. But they only come out in the evening or at night. Camel, which is called the ship of the desert, carries people through the desert. Did you know that the Sahara Desert is as large as the USA!

Antarctica is the largest cold desert in the world. It is completely white and is covered with snow. This desert is on the South Pole. It is the coldest place on earth. But a few animals live here. Penguins are the most famous animals that live here.

The animals and plants that live in deserts drink very little water. Animals in the deserts can go without drinking water for many days.

Let's remember the story

1. What is a desert?
2. Which is the most easily found plant in the desert?
3. What is a cold desert?
4. Who is called the ship of the desert? Why?
5. Which is the largest cold desert? Where is it?
6. Do the animals that live in the desert drink lots of water?

Think and write the correct opposite of the words given below.

1. Long

2. Dry

3. Little

4. Hot

5. Small

6. Full

 **Find friends**

Some words are given below in two columns. These words are called **rhyming words** because when you speak them, their ends sound the same. Read these words aloud and match each word with its friend.

Column A	Column B
Very	Tune
Know	Lip
Found	Berry
Dune	Hand
Sand	Low
Ship	Round

Crazy grid

Find all the words given in the box in the grid given below.

Sahara, snow, desert, dunes, cactus, camel, penguin, water

U	I	D	A	D	P	C	P	T	D
A	P	E	N	G	U	I	N	E	S
S	H	S	U	I	P	N	F	C	A
N	A	E	T	C	E	D	E	S	H
O	E	R	G	N	A	T	G	S	A
W	A	T	E	R	F	M	I	H	R
S	H	W	E	U	H	W	E	D	A
B	C	A	C	T	U	S	M	L	S

Deserts on a map

The teacher will show the children the world's physical map with the deserts marked on it. She will then tell the students about deserts. She can tell them especially about Sahara Desert, about how big it is.

She will then give the children world physical maps with the outline of the deserts marked on them. Then she will ask the students to fill colour into the deserts marked on the map.

Fun to Know

A warming up discussion
What time do you get up in the morning?
What early morning sounds you hear when you wakeup?

Bed in Summer
by Robert Louis Stevenson

In Winter I get up at night

And dress by yellow candle light.

In Summer, quite the other way,

I have to go to bed by day.

I have to go to bed and see

The birds still hopping on the tree,

Or hear the grown-up people's feet

Still going past me in the street.

And does it not seem hard to you,

When all the sky is clear and blue,

And I should like so much to play,

To have to go to bed by day?

Let's remember the story

1. When does the narrator get up during winters?
2. When does the narrator go to bed during summer?
3. What does he sees when he goes to bed?
4. Where are the people walking?
5. What does he want to do when he goes to bed during summer?
6. Is the narrator happy to go to bed during day?

Just opposites

Think and write the correct opposite of the words given below.

1. Below

2. Bright

3. Careful

4. Get

5. Junior

6. Powerful

Jumbled sentences

Read the sentences given below. The words in these sentences are put wrongly. Rewrite the words to make meaningful sentences.

1. sitting / the / tree / on / is / bird / the

2. playing / the / are / children

3. beautiful / it / is / day / a

4. is / dress / Rita / a / pink / wearing

5. bee / flower / the / on / the / sitting / is

6. I / rainbow / to / see / the / like

Read aloud

Read the passage below.

Henry and his family were preparing to go camping. Then it started to rain. Henry's family could not go camping. Everyone was sad. Henry had an idea! He put up his tent in the living room. Then he put out the lights. He took out a flashlight. In its light, he put a heater near the tent. Henry and his parents sat around the heater. They ate sandwiches. Mother melted marshmallows in the microwave and then they ate them. Father told them stories. Henry was so happy. Also, there were no mosquitoes inside! Camping inside was fun. Henry and his parents had a great time.

Fun to Know

14

A warming up discussion

Have you ever skated?
Do you know about the different kinds of roller skates?

Roller Skates

A Roller Skate is a pair of shoe that has a fixed pair of rollers attached to the sole. It was after a long time and many efforts later that the present day roller skates came into being. It was no easy task but then man has always wanted to travel faster and with least effort.

John Merlin was the first person who had invented roller skates. He had done so in the 1760s in London, England. His skates were, however, not at all flexible. He even wore the skates that he had invented to a party where he crashed into a mirror hurting himself badly. After this incident, it was a long time before someone else thought of making roller skates.

Then, in 1819, Monsieur Petitbled had a patent to make a roller skate. He had invented an in-line skate with a wooden sole, leather straps and it had three wheels. His skates, however, only went forwards. It was with great difficulty that one could turn at corners.

By 1863, the roller skates had became a popular feature of the London stage. Actors used to wear skates while they acted on stage. But these skates would not turn or stop correctly. It was then that James Leonard Plimpton redesigned the roller skates. He even had a patent passed for his new design of roller skates.

His designed roller skates had four wheels and they could turn. He had made turning easy by adding a rubber cushion in the roller skate. The rubber cushion allowed the person skating to move in the direction he wanted to go in by leaning to one side. These improved skates soon became popular. It was in no time that a skating rink was opened in New York City. With time more and more improvements were made in the design of roller skates. It was done to make the roller skates more comfortable.

With time, roller skating kept on becoming popular. It became so popular that skating rinks were opened all over North America. Some restaurants even had their waiters and waitresses put on roller skates when they came to take orders. By now, skating rinks also began to play music and had disco lights to make skating fun.

Then in 1980, two Minnesota brothers, Scott and Brennan Olsen, further modified the design of the roller skates. They found an old pair of roller skates that had two pairs of four wheels below the frame. In their parent's basement they worked hard to improve the skates further. In the end, they placed the wheels in one single line below the frame of the skates. The number of wheels could be four or five. This design became popular with hockey players and soon everyone wanted to wear the roller skates with the newest design. And so it is to this day.

Let's remember the story

1. Who had first invented the roller skates?
2. What happened when he went to a party?
3. How could the skates designed by James Leonard Plimpton move?
4. Where do people go to skate?
5. How was skating made fun?
6. What was different about the wheels designed by the Olsen Brothers?

Just opposites

Think and write the correct opposite of the words given below.

1. More

2. Open

3. Easy

4. Stop

5. New

6. Light

Practice writing sentences

Make sentences of the words given below.

1. Play

2. Music

3. Pair

4. Four

5. Line

6. Stop

Words and their meanings

In the two columns given below words with their meanings are placed. But the meanings are jumbled up. Can the match the word with its correct meaning?

Word	Meaning
Invent	A floor below the ground
Flexible	To make better
Renowned	To make something new
Improve	Hard to do
Basement	To bend without breaking
Difficult	To be famous

Can you guess the word?

The letters in the words given below are all jumbled up. Put the letters in the right order to make meaningful words.

1. R E L O R L

2. K S N T I A G

3. N I R K

4. N I V T N E

5. G I E D S N

6. S T A N B E M E

Fun to Know

A warming up discussion
Did you know that rocks deep below our earth move?
Have you taken part in a disaster drill?

Earthquake

You must have felt a sudden shaking of the earth sometimes. If you have than you have felt an earthquake. Earthquakes are the shaking and rolling of the earth's surface. They take place when large rocks under the earth's surface make powerful movements.

Did you know that below the earth's surface are huge pieces of rocks! These pieces of rocks are always moving. These rocks are either going apart from each other, moving towards each other or going past each other. As these pieces of rocks move, they put pressure on each other.

When this pressure becomes too much, it is suddenly released. This released pressure causes an earthquake.

Take a pencil. Now, apply pressure with your fingers at both ends of the pencil. You will notice that the pencil will bend. And as you continue to put pressure at both ends, the pencil actually breaks. The same thing happens when there is an earthquake.

Did you know that all earthquakes take place along the boundaries of these huge rocks! The boundaries of these huge rocks have cracks in them. These cracks are called faults. As the rocks continue to push or pull, the pressure in these rocks builds up. When this pressure in the rocks is released, it moves towards the surface of the earth in the form of waves. These waves are called seismic waves. Seismic waves can travel for many kilometres.

In United States, there is a place where one can see a crack or fault in the earth's surface. This crack is called the **San Andreas Fault**. This crack is near San Francisco. Two huge rocks are moving in opposite directions along this crack. Many earthquakes have happened due to this crack.

Earthquakes are a force of nature. One cannot tell when an earthquake will take place. But as the pieces of rock continue to move, and the pressure builds up, an earthquake can take place anytime.

Let's remember the story

1. What is an earthquake?
2. Why does the earth's surface move?
3. What happens when these huge pieces of rocks move?
4. What are the cracks called?
5. Which waves travel to the surface of the earth?
6. Which crack is visible on the earth's surface?

Find friends

Some words are given below in two columns. These words are called **rhyming words** because when you speak them, their ends sound the same. Read these words aloud and match each word with its friend.

Column A	Column B
Rock	Send
Piece	Fast
Past	Block
Move	Cave
Bend	Niece
Wave	Groove

Sharing experiences

Can you tell us what you saw around yourself when you experienced an earthquake? Tell us how you felt? Were you scared? What did you do? Where were you? What did you see?

....

....

....

....

....

....

....

....

....

....

....

Practice writing sentences

Make sentences of the words given below.

1. Piece

2. Rock

3. Pencil

4. Push

5. Wave

6. Crack

Let's be safe!

Quake safe

The teacher can tell the students about an earthquake. She can tell them what they must do if they are living in an earthquake prone zone. She can tell them how they can make themselves safe, what they must do, if they can, to help others in need.

Fun to Know

A warming up discussion

Did you know that foxes are sly?
Have you played a trick on your friend?

Little Red Hen

Once, there lived a Little Red Hen alone in a small house on a tree. Every time the Little Red Hen went out, she would lock the door. She always kept a pair of scissors, a thread and a needle in her apron pocket.

On a nearby hill lived a Sly Fox. For long, the Sly Fox had wanted to eat the Little Red Hen. He had tried hard but had not been successful in his attempts.

One day, the Sly Fox thought of a trick. 'Today, I will definitely catch the Little Red Hen and eat her for dinner,' he said to himself. Then, he took a sack and a rope and rushed out of his house.

Soon, the Sly Fox reached the Little Red Hen's house. He hid behind a big tree near the hen's house. Soon, the Little Red Hen opened the door to her house and climbed down the ladder. 'I must gather firewood, quickly,' she said. Quickly, she began collecting wood. But today, she forgot to close the door to her house. The Sly Fox saw it and without waiting rushed inside the Little Red Hen's house. Once inside, he hid behind the door. Minutes later, the Little Red Hen returned with the wood. She put the wood near the fireplace.

Then, as she was closing the door, she saw the Sly Fox.

'I caught you at last, Little Red Hen,' said the Sly Fox.

The Little Red Hen was frightened. She fluttered her wings and flew to the top of the cupboard. Once there, she cried, 'You will never catch me, Sly Fox.'

'Oh! That was clever, Little Red Hen but I will surely catch you today,' replied the Sly Fox. He had thought of another trick. Then, the Sly Fox started running around in circles at great speed. In no time, seeing the circular movement of the Sly Fox, the Little Red Hen became dizzy and fell down from the cupboard. Quickly, the Sly Fox caught the Little Red Hen and put her into the sack he had bought.

Then, he tied the opening of the sack with a rope. Then, smirking to himself, the Sly Fox went towards his house. Now, it was a hot day. As the

Sly Fox climbed up the hill, he soon became tired. 'I must rest a while,' thought the Sly Fox. Thinking thus, he lay down under a tree and soon he was fast asleep.

As the Sly Fox slept, the Little Red Hen woke up. When she found herself inside a sack, she understood everything. 'I must get out of here before the Sly Fox wakes up,' thought the Little Red Hen. Then, the clever hen took out her scissors and made a hole in the sack. Through that hole, she stepped out of the sack. Then, she quickly filled the sack with stones and sewed it with needle and thread. Then smiling to herself, the Little Red Hen ran towards her house.

Soon, she had returned home. Meanwhile, the Sly Fox woke up. 'I must be going along,' he said and picking up the sack went to his house. Soon, the Sly Fox reached his house. He then put a pot on fire, filled it with water and then put vegetables in it.

When the water had started boiling, the Sly Fox opened the sack and upturned it over the vessel. The next moment, the stones inside the sack fell into the pot and boiling water splashed all over the Sly Fox's face. The Sly Fox cried out in pain as his face was covered in boils. After that day, the Sly Fox never tried to catch the Little Red Hen. He had learnt his lesson.

 **Let's remember the story**

1. Where did the Little Red Hen live?
2. What did she always have in her pocket?
3. Where did the Sly Fox hide?
4. What did the Sly fox do to catch the Little Red Hen?
5. How did the Little Red Hen fill the sack?
6. What did happen when rocks fell into the pot?

 Gender bender

Can you give the opposite gender of the given words?

Column A	Column B
Hen	
Lion	
Fox	
Deer	
Horse	
Sheep	

 Complete the sentences

Read the sentences below. Complete them using the correct words from the brackets.

1. The boy carried a.................. (bag/ sack) to school.
2. Toby is riding his..................... (bicycle/ bus).
3. The hens are eating.................. (grains/ eggs).
4. Cars are running on the................ (track/ road).
5. Water is coming out of the............... (tap/ roof).

Read aloud

Read the passage given below aloud!

Hummingbirds are the world's smallest birds. The smallest Hummingbird called the Bee Hummingbird is only 2 inches long!

Its wings shine and glitter in the sun. Did you know that a hummingbird beats its wings very, very fast! This tiny bird can be red, blue, green, violet or golden in colour. Hummingbirds drink the nectar of flowers. It does so by using its long bill. It inserts its bill inside flowers to drink nectar. Did I mention that Hummingbirds are the only birds in the world that can fly backwards! These tiny birds also like the colour red and are attracted to it.